A STRAIGHTFORWARD GUIDE TO SPEECH WRITING AND PRESENTATION

R WATSON
STRAIGHTFORWARD PUBLISHING

Straightforward Publishing
38 Cromwell Road
Walthamstow
London E17 9JN

© R. Watson 1998
First edition 1998

All rights reserved. No part of this publication may be reproduced in a retrieval system or transmitted by any means, electronic or mechanical, photocopying or otherwise, without the prior permission of the copyright holder.

British Library cataloguing in Publication Data. A catalogue record is available for this book from the British Library.

ISBN 1899924 51 5

Printed and Bound by BPC Information Ltd

Cover design by Straightforward Graphics

Whilst every effort has been taken to ensure that the information in this book is accurate at the time of going to press, the author and publishers recognise that the information can become out of date. The book is therefore sold on the condition that no responsibility for errors or omissions is assumed. The author and publisher cannot be held liable for any information contained within.

A Straightforward Guide to Speech Writing and Presentation

CONTENTS

INTRODUCTION

1. Giving a speech-knowing your audience 9

2. Public Speaking Generally 17

3. Researching, planning and writing a speech 23

4. Presentation skills 31

5. The use of visual aids 41

6. Effective delivery-the voice 49

7. The usefulness of exercises prior to speaking 61

8. Delivering your presentation 67

9. Different events 71

   Compere/Master of Ceremonies 79
   After dinner speeches
   Weddings
   Impromptu speaking
   Keynote speeches

INTRODUCTION

This book is designed for those who find public speaking and presenting in front of others a nerve wracking experience and who wish to gain more knowledge concerning the art of speech writing.

There are a number of key aspects which are fundamental to the art of Speech writing and making presentations. Without a doubt the two most important are the person presenting and the nature of the material. This book concentrates heavily on these areas, offering invaluable advice.

In addition, advice on the use of visual aids and on the nature of the setting in which the public speaker will deliver his or her address is offered and also instruction on making the presentation and audience management.

Overall, this book will benefit those people who are new to the area of speech writing, public speaking and making presentations. However, it will also benefit those who are more experienced but need a refresher.

There are key points at the end of each chapter which help to reinforce the main areas.

Effective speech writing and public speaking is an art and a skill and the rewards to those who can become effective presenters are enormous. It is hoped that this book will go some way to developing the skills and abilities needed.

CHAPTER ONE
DELIVERING A SPEECH- KNOWING YOUR AUDIENCE

The first thing to consider when accepting an invitation to speak is the nature and type of the function in question and also the type of audience that you will be addressing. This is absolutely essential for anyone who is being called on to deliver a speech.

Following this, you will need to set objectives for yourself and to create a framework for your speech based around those objectives. This is the essential starting point for all speech writing and presenting.

Objectives fall into several categories:

- The need to entertain your audience and to warm them to you

- The need to pass on essential information

- The need to fire your audience, to inspire them

- The need to persuade the audience

- The need to open up debate.

Defining your objectives

The main objective is the one that you want to achieve in the best of circumstances. *The main or primary objective is the one which is your main concern.* Therefore, it is essential that you have this key objective at the core of what it is you are formulating.

Whether your main objective when delivering a speech is to inform, persuade or entertain, it is essential that you provoke some sort of reaction from your audience. When this happens, you have succeeded in your task. You have fulfilled your purpose as a speaker.

Formulating objectives

You need to consider very carefully the task that you have in hand. Basically, you have to speak to a particular type of audience about a given subject on a particular occasion. Formulate a statement of objectives at this point and write it down succinctly.

Include secondary objectives in addition to primary objectives. It may be your main objective to impart information and inform, in certain circumstances. However, a secondary objective may be to entertain. At least, if the audience is entertained then you will have achieved something. Essentially, in all speeches, you should aim to entertain. This will leave people with a good feeling and not an empty feeling, a feeling that time has been wasted.

Knowing your audience

There is one main golden rule when speaking in public. Always keep your audience in the forefront of your mind. Always meet the expectation of your audience. The speech must be tailored to suit the needs of the audience and to suit their level. Use language that they will understand.

DELIVERING A SPEECH-KNOWING YOUR AUDIENCE

You will need essential information about your audience. The following should be considered:

- What is the make up of the audience?

- What is the age group?

- What is their interest in the event?

- What economic group are they from?

- What racial and cultural background are they from?

- Are they attending voluntarily or involuntarily?

Write down what it is that you think your audience are interested in and why they are attending the event at which you will be making a speech. Then you will be in a position to decide how your subject and your objectives can marry with what you think are the interests of the audience.

Audiences can be categorized and profiled in terms of their background and their varying levels of expertise. Some audiences are drawn from a profession and others are non expert audiences. It very much depends on the occasion. Are you addressing a professional gathering or are you at a social gathering, such as a wedding? Each occasion will differ and, even before you can consider writing a speech you must carry out thorough research into the audience and the desired outcomes of what it is you are trying to put across.

Write down what you think your audiences level of expertise is likely to be, and then decide how this will affect your speech.

Every audience has a profile of expertise and its own interests in being at an event. One of the fundamental objectives is to join an audience in its common interest and convey your message in a way that can be understood. The key is to gain the audiences attention and to make them ready to listen to what you have to say. A little later in the book we will be looking at techniques when public speaking.

If we examine audience needs a little further, psychologists believe that people nowadays have a number of needs and that they are fundamentally the same in everyone. These are:

- Economic needs

- The need for physical comfort

- The need to be free from worry and anxiety

- The need to be accepted by others

- The need to explore new ideas

- The need to be free from political oppression.

Each member of an audience has these needs and they expect the speaker to fulfill at least one of the needs or indicate how they may do so. It is essential that you fulfill the audiences expectations if your speech is to be successful.

You should assemble everything that you know about your audience, putting together your perceptions about their particular interests, their reasons for attending and their level of expertise and reason for attending the speech. When you have successfully joined the needs and level of your audience with your stated objectives, then you will have completed the necessary pre-planning work which is vital to the construction of a good and effective speech. The next stage is to start to construct the speech. However, before we consider this stage, we will explore some of the general concepts and practices of public speaking in a little more depth.

Now read the key points from chapter one.

KEY POINTS FROM CHAPTER ONE

- The first thing to consider when accepting an invitation to speak is the nature and type of the function in question and also the type of audience

- Following this consideration, you will need to set objectives for yourself and create a framework for your speech.

CHAPTER TWO

PUBLIC SPEAKING GENERALLY

Before looking at the crafting of a speech, based on what we have been discussing, we need to look at public speaking generally. It is only when you learn the art of public speaking that you can become an accomplished speaker and, by definition, deliver an effective speech. It is very much more than just standing up and talking to others, as you will probably have started to gather.

Public speaking is very much an art and a skill which can be mastered by anyone. It is true to say that some people may be initially better equipped for the role of public speaker than others, by virtue of their own particular personality type. However, the truly effective public speaker learns the craft and applies certain techniques which generally derive from experience.

In this book I will be alluding to the person who has to deliver a speech or present a seminar, rather than the professional teacher. It is the person who is not constantly engaged in addressing groups who will most benefit from what is contained within.

The person and the material

There are two vital ingredients in public speaking. The first is very much the person delivering the speech or other material to a group. The second is the nature of the material being delivered.

The Person

For some people, standing in front of an audience, whatever the size, is not a real problem. For others however, the very thought of exposing oneself to a group of people, and being so vulnerable, is a nightmare best avoided.

When trying to put this into context it is important to remember that, when we communicate as part of a group, or simply on a one to one basis with another, then we interact primarily through speech and body language. We are often confident within ourselves because we feel secure in that we are part of a group interacting and that all eyes are not on us alone, at least not for a protracted period.

The situation is very different indeed when we are alone and faced with a group of people, strangers or not, and we have to present material. It means that we have to assume responsibility and take the lead and communicate successfully to others. Nervousness is very often the result when placed in this situation because, until we can make contact with the audience and establish a rapport, we are very much alone and feel vulnerable.

Obviously, there are a number of factors influencing the levels of confidence and differences in attitude between people, such as the nature and type of the person and their background, their past experience, both within the family and in the world of work and numerous other experiences besides. All these will affect a persons ability to become an effective public speaker.

This publication cannot completely erase your nervousness. It cannot change your personality overnight. However, what it can certainly do is to raise your awareness to the root of that feeling in the context of public speaking and to help you become more confident. It can also show you that, whatever your personality type, you can become a successful public speaker by applying certain fundamental techniques.

Why do we feel nervous?

There are a number of reasons why we may feel nervous. You need to question yourself and ask yourself why. Was the sight of so many faces in front of you enough to frighten you and make you lose your self confidence or are you plagued by the memory of previous mistakes? You need to remember that you change and develop as a person as you gain more experience and that past mistakes do not mean that you will repeat them.

Lets face it, most of us will experience nerves in a situation which is stressful to us. This is totally normal and quite often we become anxious and charged with adrenaline which drives us on. When it comes to speaking in public the adrenaline can be positive but excessive nerves are negative and can lead to aggression.

Fundamentally, the key to successful public speaking is the acquisition of confidence coupled with assertiveness which leads to the ability to effectively control a situation. If you are assertive and you know your subject matter you are likely to be confident and in control and less likely to feel nervous.

Be prepared!

Directly related to the above, preparation is everything and to feel confident with your material means that you are half way there already. Although I will be expanding on preparation a little later, there are a few fundamental tips which can help you along.

You should listen to speakers, particularly good speakers as often as possible in order to gain tips. Notice the way that good and effective speakers construct their sentences. Listen for the eloquence. Remember, shorter sentences have a lot more impact and are easier to grasp than long sentences. They also act a discipline for the speaker in that they will prevent him or her from straying off the point.

Another very important tip when approaching the day of your presentation is preparing yourself psychologically. Convince yourself that you are looking forward to the speech and that you will do well no matter what. Convey this to your audience as you open your presentation, say that you are glad to be with them and that you hope that this goes well for all. This reinforces a feeling of goodwill and will express itself through your body language and your voice.

Finally, one of the main aids to effective public speaking is *experience* and that only comes through practice so it is essential that you take every opportunity offered you to sharpen your skills in this area.

In the next chapter I will be concentrating on presentation and style. Fundamental to preparation as a speaker is the ability to relax and focus your mind and body on the task ahead.

Now read the key points from Chapter two overleaf.

KEY POINTS FROM CHAPTER TWO

- The truly effective public speaker learns the craft and applies certain techniques which generally derive from experience

- There are two vital ingredients in public speaking. The first is the person and the second is the material

- The key to successful public speaking is the acquisition of knowledge coupled with assertiveness which leads to the ability to control and direct a situation

- Listen to effective and successful speakers in order to gain tips

- Prepare yourself psychologically for your speech. Put yourself in a positive frame of mind!

CHAPTER THREE
RESEARCHING, PLANNING AND WRITING A SPEECH

The key to speech preparation is research, thorough research. Take research very seriously because audiences can tell very quickly what level of preparation you are at. The type of occasion will determine the level and type of research.

Whatever the type of occasion, you should have developed a little library of information and have this at your fingertips. There are a number of sources of information, which again will vary depending on the type of occasions:

Libraries.

The local library should be your starting point. There are many works of reference and in addition libraries are invaluable sources of other information, such as where you can go to develop your subject, any associations that may exist and so on.

Newspapers and magazines

Local and national newspapers are indispensable sources of information. Trade magazines will inform you about a particular profession and other papers, such as freepapers, should not be overlooked. You should begin to develop a cuttings file that you can dip into as and when the occasion is right.

Radio and television

Invaluable again. You should have a notebook waiting by your radio or TV so that you can jot down anything of interest.

Reference books

Good reference books, such as the Guinness book of records and English dictionaries, plus thesaurus are essential for research.

In addition, specialist organizations and other areas where experts tend to gather are very important indeed.

You should file your material and ensure that you have checked the facts before you put together a speech. When and if you use statistics and figures, check them and quote your sources. Make sure that you get it right on the day. Avoid any slander against another. Do not be unprofessional when including facts and figures. Audiences tend to see speakers who indulge in slander as negative and tend to turn away quite quickly.

Planning and writing a speech

When it comes to planning, it is better to have too much material than too little. Ensure that your research is derived from your own personal experience, as much as possible, rather than simply cold hard facts.

A successful speech utilizes a relatively small amount of information, which is chosen for its relevance to the audience and for its usefulness in achieving the objectives of the speaker. Different people have different methods of planning speeches. However, most people will engage in some sort of brainstorming. This involves scribbling down often random thoughts. Brainstorming is useful in that it will produce, after a while, a train of thoughts.

Definition of the topic

Speech writing should be a process of simplification rather than complication. The key is to sort through the mass of material and whittle it down until you have a small, well defined topic upon which to speak. You will achieve this by writing down words or phrases that cover the subject you want to tackle. Then choose a list of topics that fall into this subject field. Choose the one that most relates to your audiences needs and expectations, and is most likely to enable you to fulfill your objectives. Again, write down a list of sub topics under your chosen topic heading, and choose one that fits with the context.

Composing the title of a speech

Some organizers require that you let them have a title of your speech in advance. This enables them to include it in the forthcoming program. When you have defined your topic and sorted the information you have you should then be able to think of a title.

Your title should be concise and catchy and it should also make your speech sound interesting. The aim is to get people to come and hear you speak.

Structuring a speech

A good speech is pieced together in a defined structure and contains a number of specific elements. The structure of a speech should comprise the following:

- The opening. This is where the speaker needs to grab the attention of the audience

- Introduction to the subject. This is where the speaker gives an overview of the material to be covered

- The body of the speech. This is where the speaker presents information or arguments

- Close. This is where the speaker draws conclusions from the information already presented and leaves the audience with something to think about.

Although most compositions have a beginning, middle and end speeches can differ somewhat. The most important difference between a speech and other presentations is that a speech is fleeting, it is uttered and then disappears. It is not possible for a listener of a speech to go back to the beginning if they are not paying attention. At least not during the speech, maybe after with a transcript. The good speech writer will therefore build in elements so that the audience is kept alert. These elements are:

- Splashes. These are attention grabbers which surprise people and gain their interest right at the beginning

- Appeals. These are where sentences identify the speakers purpose with the needs of the audience

- Links. These are sentences that link one piece of argument to the next in a logical manner.

It is easier to write the introduction and main body of your speech before you tackle the opening and the close. You will write a more effective opening and close if you deal with them together at the end of the writing process.

- Summaries and repetitions. These are useful techniques to ensure that the audience follows the argument and remembers as much as possible after you have stepped out of the limelight. The general rule is: tell them what you are going to tell them; tell them; and then tell them what you have told them.

Openings

When a speaker starts to speak, or rises to begin to speak, the audience will appraise him or her on the physical appearance. The second critical moment is when the first words are uttered. Apart from the formal address, the elements to build into the opening are: a splash, an appeal and credentials, followed by a statement of the topic on which you are going to speak. The splash is a method of grabbing the audiences attention. Choose a splash that is relevant and also topical. Once the audience is paying attention, make them see that your topic is not only interesting, but also relevant to their experience and needs.

Next, prove to the audience that you are someone who has something interesting and worthwhile to say, and that your facts can be relied upon. State your credentials, then give a short sharp simple explanation of what it is that you are going to talk about, and what you hope to achieve by doing so. These last two elements, the statement of your subject and your objectives should be, in effect, a promise to go some way towards fulfilling the audiences needs.

A strong opening should be confident, friendly, short and simple. The speaker who apologizes or who undermines his/herself will lose respect immediately. On the other hand, a long rambling opening will confuse and irritate, boding no good for the rest of the speech.

Introduction

When you have completed the arrangement of the material, you should have a series of headings that lead from one another logically. Under each of these headings you will have a number of pieces of material to utilize. During the introduction, you need to set out for the audience the main elements of your argument. State each of the headings in the order in which you are going to present them, and explain what they mean. Tell the audience what it is that you are going to tell them.

Closing a speech

It is a fact that most audiences have a very short time span. They are generally attentive at the start of a presentation, but after a few minutes their concentration begins to waver. However, they will usually perk up again towards the end of the speech. The close of the speech is just as important as the opening and it is up to the speaker to make sure that the audience attention is held.

The close should be a short summary of all the material that you covered in your presentation, and you should draw any conclusion from the arguments that you have presented. In this way you will repeat the salient points that you wished to put across, and the audience is likely to remember some of what you have said.

Always end on a high note and try to leave the audience with words that sum up your speech. Above all, make sure that you close confidently and that your audience know that the speech is over. Avoid at all cost the pregnant pause or the embarrassed silence.

Now read the key points from chapter three overleaf.

KEY POINTS FROM CHAPTER THREE

- The key to speech preparation is thorough research. The type of occasion will determine the level and type of research

- In order to facilitate research you should develop a comprehensive library of information

- When it comes to planning it is better to have too much information than too little

- Speech writing is, above all, a process of simplification. You should sift through all your material until you have a well defined topic which is not over laden with information.

CHAPTER FOUR

PRESENTATION SKILLS

Having looked at preparation for speech writing and also structuring a speech, it is now necessary to consider some more specific points connected with presentation of a speech.

Personal skills

Body Language

People have a natural ability to use body language together with speech. Body language emphasises speech and enables us to communicate more effectively with others. It is vitally important when preparing for the role of public speaker to understand the nature of your body language and also to connect this to another all important element-*vision*.

Vision

People tend to take in a lot of information with their eyes and obviously presentations are greatly enhanced by use of visual aids. Together, when presenting to a group of people, as a public speaker, *body language and visual stimuli* are all important. A great amount of thought needs to go into the elements of what it is that you are about to present and the way you intend to convey your message. What you should not do, especially as a novice, is to stand up in front of a group and deliver a presentation off the top of your head. You need to carry out thorough research into what it is you are presenting and to whom you are presenting.

Developing a style

Every person engaged in public speaking will have his or her own style. At the one end of the spectrum there are those people who give no thought to what it is they are doing and have no real interest in the audience. For them it is a chore and one which should be gotten over as soon as is possible. Such public speakers can be slow, boring and ineffectual leaving only traces of annoyance in the audiences mind. Here, there is a definite absence of style.

At the other end of the spectrum are those who have given a great deal of thought to what they are doing, given a great deal of thought to their material and have a genuine interest in the audience. Such public speakers will be greatly stimulating and leave a lasting impression and actually convey something of some worth.

It does not matter what the occasion of your public speaking role is, wedding (best mans speech etc.) seminar, presentation to employers. The principles are the same-that is understanding your material, understand the nature of yourself as you relate to the material and how this will translate into spoken and body language and also how you will use visual aids to enhance the presentation.

Underlying all of this is your *own personal style*, partly which develops from an understanding of the above and partly from an understanding of yourself. Some presenters of material recognise their own speed of presentation, i.e. slow, medium or fast and also understand their own body language. Some are more fluent than others, use their hands more etc. Having recognized your own style what you need to do is to adjust your own way of presentation to the specific requirements of the occasion. The key point is to gain attention, get the message across and be stimulating to a degree. Obviously some occasions are more formal than others. You should study the nature of the occasion and give a lot of thought to what is required, i.e. degree of humor, seriousness etc. All of the above considerations begin to translate themselves into a style which you yourself will begin to recognize and feel comfortable with. Once this occurs you will find that, when presenting, your nerves will begin to melt away and your confidence begins to develop

Presentations

As this is a book about speech writing, and also presentation, we should now concentrate on the various elements which go to make up a successful presentation to a group.

There is not one particular style appropriate to public speaking. Each occasion will merit its own approach. However, there are a few commonly observed rules.

Use of language

The use of language is a specific medium which must be understood when making a presentation. Obviously, if you are speaking publicly to a group of familiar people who know and understand you, a different approach will be needed and a different form of language, perhaps less formal, utilized than that used in front of a group who are totally unfamiliar.

Nevertheless, using formal but simple language interspersed with funny remarks is undoubtedly one of the best ways to approach any form of audience, friends or not. You should certainly avoid too much detail and do not go overboard with funny comments as this will become tedious. Stick to the subject matter lightening up the occasion with a few anecdotes and witty comments. It is all about the right blend and pitch.

Body Language

We have briefly discussed body language. It is astounding how much you can tell about people in the street by simply observing their body language. Usually people form an impression about another within the first five minutes of meeting. It is essential, in a public speaking situation that your body language should reflect a confident personality with a good sense of humor. In order to achieve this you should think about the following:

Use of hands

- Use your hands to emphasize what you say and to invite the audience to accept your point

- Keep your hands open and keep your fingers open.

- Avoid putting your hands in your pocket and avoid closing them. Firmly avoid pointing fingers

- co-ordinate your hand movements with your words.

Using facial expressions

People tend to concentrate on the face of a public speaker, in addition to the movements of the body. Obviously, your face, along with body language is a vehicle for expression. A smile every now and again is important. There are other actions which can help:

- Use of eyebrows for inviting people to accept your ideas

- Moving the head to look at all members of a group. Very important indeed to maintain a sense of involvement on the part of all

- Do not fix your eyes on one place or person for long. This will isolate the rest of the audience and may be interpreted as nervousness or a lack of confidence on your part

- Look at individuals every time you mention something in their area of expertise or are singling them out in a positive way

- Look at people even if they appear not to be looking at you

The face is a very important part of the communication apparatus and the use of this part of the body is of the utmost importance when public speaking.

Controlling your movements

In addition to the use of face and hands the way you move can have an effect on your audience. Your movements can vary from standing rigid and fixed to acting out roles and being fluid generally. There are, in keeping with body language generally, certain rules relating to movement:

- Restrict your movements only to those which are most necessary. Avoid throwing yourself all over the place and distracting peoples attention from the emphasis of your presentation

- Always face the people that you are addressing. Never look at the floor or away from the audience, at least not for a prolonged period of time

Dress

When adopting the role of public speaker it is very important to be dressed formally and in accordance with the standard of the occasion, or the nature of the occasion. Dressing formally does not mean automatically wearing a suit and tie. It does mean however that you should think in terms of power dressing. This means that you wish to make an impression on people, not just through what you say and do, not just through your body language or visual presentations but by the way you look. People must be impressed. This means that you must give thought to what you wear, how you can help to achieve a sense of control through dress.

Attitude

Your attitude is crucial to your success in public speaking. Attitudes can be greatly influenced by nerves and by being ill prepared. There is nothing worse than a public speaker who slowly degenerates into aggression or hostility through sarcasm or other forms of attack. Yet this is all too frequent. At all times you must maintain a professional and formal attitude which allows you to remain in control. You can think yourself into this state if you find yourself slipping or feel that you are losing control.

If you feel that you are straying in any way then you should get back on course. This can be achieved through a number of ways such as by changing the subject slightly in order to give yourself time to gather your wits or by asking the group to refocus on the subject in question.

Attitude is also disciplined by self composure which can be engendered through relaxation which in turn is brought about by understanding the role of exercise and meditation, which we will be elaborating on a little later.

Formalities

Another fundamental rule of presentations is the way you open or introduce the presentation and the way you close. When public speaking it is always necessary to introduce yourself even if most of the audience know who you are. It is vital that everyone knows who you are, who you represent, if anybody, and what you are there for.

Having got these necessary formalities over with the audience will feel more comfortable listening to you because they now have a point of reference.

Depending on the situation, you may even want to ask the audience if they would like to introduce themselves, through a "round robin" which entails each person telling you and the others who they are and what they hope to get out of the presentation. This approach however, is only really necessary and useful in seminar or teaching situations. Such an approach would be wholly inappropriate in a speech situation.

Practicing presentations

Taking into account all of the above and then practicing. This is the absolute key to successful presentations and to effective public speaking. Practice most certainly lifts your confidence level up and assists you in staying in control The more time and effort that you spend practicing the less that you will have to worry about when presenting. Lets face it, a presentation is a live stage show. How do stand up comics feel when they expose themselves to an audience? Develop a practicing technique by trying different methods:

- You should choose a topic that you are very interested in and prepare a short presentation on it.

- Stand in front of a mirror and present to yourself. Repeat this over and over observing different aspects of your style.

- Try to rectify any bad habits.

- Experiment with various styles and techniques until you find one that suits you.

- Try to film yourself if possible. Replay the film and observe yourself. This is one of the most effective ways of changing your style, or developing your style.

- Ask a friend to observe you and to make detailed criticism. Do not be afraid of criticism as this is always constructive

At this point you should be concentrating on style only. Do not worry about content as we will be discussing this a little later.

Now read the key points from chapter two.

KEY POINTS FROM CHAPTER TWO

- Body language emphasises speech and helps us to communicate more effectively with others

- Visual stimuli is equally as important when public speaking

- It is very important to develop your own style as a public speaker

- The use of language is a specific medium which must be understood when public speaking

- Formal but simple language interspersed with funny remarks is one of the best ways to approach an audience

- The use of facial expressions is very important when addressing others

- The way you move can have a very important effect on an audience

- Adopt an appropriate mode of dress for the audience you are addressing. It is better to be smart than scruffy

- Your attitude is crucial to your success as a public speaker

- The way you open and close your presentation is of the utmost importance

- You should always practice presentations before the event

CHAPTER FIVE

THE USE OF VISUAL AIDS

Before we further discuss presentation of your material it is necessary to talk a little about the use of visual aids. Although many speeches are carried out without the use of visuals, it is surprising what a difference they can make.

When making a speech, visual aids are used for effect, for helping you to make your point. They offer audiences a visual representation of what you are trying to put across. Generally, you can explain a point much quicker with the use of such aids.

Visual aids also keep audiences interested as there is more entertainment value with the use of visual images than there is with the spoken word. Combined with words, visual aids help you to communicate ideas in a very short time and leave a longer lasting impression on the audience. This is only true, though, if you use them to their best effect. The opposite can have a detrimental effect on the audience.

Visual aids are not effective if they are not prepared very carefully together with the script that you are presenting. Do not try to overload the visual aid in terms of its contents or this will, more often than not, confuse your audience. Whether you use a graph, diagram or picture on the slide (if it is a slide that you are using) then put only one on each slide. When working on the main body of the slide keep the following in mind:

- Keep it as simple as possible

- Use pictures as often as you can keeping text to a minimum

- Leave plenty of space between items for visibility

- Use professional images (computer generated) as opposed to hand drawn.

Throughout your presentation, try to use the same style for visual aids.

Presenting with visual images

Images are there to help you and you should be comfortable with using the equipment which displays them. The following tips are useful when presenting:

- Ignore the existence of a picture behind you. Never turn your back on the audience. Talk to them at the same time as they are looking at the image

- Always rehearse with your visual aids. This will help you to familiarize yourself with the equipment and also to remember the sequence in which you will present the slides

- If you are going to use an overhead projector, make sure that all your acetates are in order. Put them back in the same order when you finish so that they are ready for use the next time. Keep them clean.

- Stand to one side of the overhead projector when you are presenting. Use a pointer to make a relevant point. Let the audience see where you are pointing your pointer.

Tools for the presentation of visual aids

Use of an Overhead projector

This particular tool is the most popular of all visual aids. It is widely used in all forms of presentations because of its flexibility. It can be used to project almost any form of material.

Slide projectors

This is the second most popular tool for visual aids The quality is always very good, often much better than the OHP. However, it can be more expensive to produce materials than the OHP.

Using a video

This is the most effective visual aid but should be used only for limited periods. More information can be shown in a short space of time than other forms of visual aid.

Use of a monitor view pad

This is a relatively new method of projection. The device has a transparent liquid display screen which, when connected to a computer acts as a monitor. The screen can then be placed on an OHP to replace an acetate. This is slightly more technical and long winded than the OHP on its own but the results can be very professional.

Use of other visual aids

In addition to the main method chosen by yourself there are other peripheral visual aids which you may wish to utilize. The following are also quite effective:

- *Flip chart.* This particular tool enables you to write and draw as you go along. Also very useful if you wish people to break into groups in order to carry out an exercise.

- *models and prototypes.* Showing a model is very powerful when trying to demonstrate a particular point. Displaying models of buildings can be more effective than showing plans.

Use of color

Color is also a very powerful medium when you wish to make important information stand out. The audience can focus on the colored parts with the background information remaining in the background.

Working with computers

Computers are playing an increasingly important part in presentations. Whether you are making or presenting slides, the results look more professional and effective with the use of presentation or graphics software.

Choosing the right equipment

It is important to use the right kind of visual aids for each occasion. If used incorrectly, visual aids can give the wrong impression or even ruin your chances of success in getting your message across. Choosing the right visual aid is quite difficult. The following are points to consider:

- The ability to grab the audiences attention. There is no point in using the most impressive equipment if it will not appeal to the audience

- The suitability for the occasion. You do not need to use state of the art equipment if you are giving a short speech. Use the most appropriate form of equipment

- The effect of your visual aids on the audience. Will the visual aid that you intend to use help or just confuse the audience. You should very carefully ensure that what you use perfectly compliments your presentation.

Use of notes and handouts

It is sometimes useful to provide your audience with a handout of your presentation, or part of your presentation. This very much depends on what you are presenting or whether you are making a simple speech. Only provide handouts when needed and not at the start of the presentation as this will distract the audience from what it is you are trying to say and also the content of any visual aid.

Involving the audience

Sometimes you may wish to involve the audience in an interactive presentation. If you need to make a quick survey or opinion poll to prove a point, you can pass a short questionnaire to the audience and let someone help you in counting the votes and presenting.

Always remember, visual aids are there to assist you in presenting your message and if they don't achieve that don't bother with them.

Now read the key points from chapter four

KEY POINTS FROM CHAPTER FOUR

- Visual aids are for effect, for helping you to make your point

- Visual aids are not effective if they are not prepared in line with the material that you are presenting

- Keep visual aids as simple as possible

- Use professional images

- When presenting, stand to one side to enable the audience to see what it is that you are presenting

- Select carefully the tool for presenting the visual aids

- The use of notes and handouts can be important in some cases

CHAPTER SIX

EFFECTIVE DELIVERY-THE VOICE

We need to consider one of the most important aspects of public speaking before we move on to actual presentation.

What you say is very important indeed. However, even more important is the way that you say it. The right combination of body language and voice is far more potent than a clever and witty script. The two combined can help you become a very effective public speaker indeed.

The voice

The voice plays a very important role in presentation and public speaking generally. The way you pitch your voice is guaranteed to either keep peoples attention or send them to sleep.

The voice is a result of air coming out of your lungs which causes the vocal chords to vibrate, producing different sounds. These various sounds are shaped into words by the speech organism in the head.

The brain then sends messages controlling the breathing and the tension of the vocal chords. Cavities in the body, such as the mouth and chest, provide amplification. The amplified sounds are then shaped into recognizable speech by the tongue, lips teeth etc. Speech is produced in two different ways:

- Voiced sounds-produced by speech organs in the mouth closer to the vocal chords at the back end of the tongue

- Unvoiced sounds-produced mainly using the tongue and front teeth. The sound of the letter S is produced in this way.

All the above aspects of voice and speech are controlled by the body organs that are unique to each person. We can develop the ability to control these organs to produce the speech that we want. This can be achieved by training the various muscles that produce and shape sounds. The shape of various cavities, such as the chest, can be changed to vary the level of sound amplification.

Developing your voice

It is perfectly possible, and probably essential to improve on four characteristics of your speech:

- tone

- pitch

- volume

- clarity.

Tone

If you restrict your body cavities responsible for amplifying sound, your voice will sound restricted and sometimes nasal. Restriction of body cavities can happen by standing or sitting in the wrong way.

It is essential that you give thought to your posture and bearing when public speaking.

Pitch

As you stretch and loosen your voice chords, the pitch of your voice will change. When stretched, the number of vibrations increases due to the small distance allowed for them to vibrate. These vibrations produce high frequency (pitch) sounds. When the vocal chords are loose, more distance is allowed for them to vibrate which makes them produce low frequency (pitch) sounds.

Volume

The volume of your voice can be improved in two ways. The first is by simply increasing the pressure of air coming out of your lungs, or by narrowing the space between the vocal chords (glottis). You can change the volume of a whisper simply by increasing the amount of air through your glottis which is widely open. Try to shout. You will notice that your glottis contracts sharply, to increase the volume of your voice.

Clarity

To get your message across you need to say it clearly. Clarity is determined by the speech organs and how well you can control them. If you are too nervous your tongue and lips start playing tricks on you because they are tense. In order to speak clearly, overcome the problems associated with speech organs and get your message across.

Don't be scared of moving your lips. Exercise your speech muscles. Make sure that you pronounce things clearly and that you carry your voice.

Voice pitch

People generally feel more comfortable listening to a deep voice, one that is well rounded and smooth. However, it is important to ensure that your voice is at your natural pitch and not forced. To find Your natural pitch, concentrate on the following exercises:

- Speak at the lowest note that feels comfortable to you

- Use a musical instrument, e,.g. a guitar or piano and find the note that corresponds to your lowest comfortable pitch

- Move four notes up the musical scale. This should be very close to your natural pitch

- Try to tune your voice with this note and speak with the music helping you to stay in tune

- Practice this as many times as you need, in order to become confident in finding your natural pitch quite quickly.

When you have found the natural pitch of your voice, you will need to work on some variations to make your speech more natural. Changing the pitch up and down according to the contents of the speech helps you to keep the audience attracted to what you are saying. Try saying a few sentences out loud and practice varying the pitch. You can then notice the relation between the contents of the sentences and your pitch when saying each of them. When you realize what you are capable of achieving with your voice, you can then consciously start varying the pitch.

Singing is very good for voice training and realizing the potential of your voice organs. Reading out loud and trying to act a story is also good training.

Use of silences and pauses

Sometimes, silence can be more effective than words. It is useful to pause every now and again to allow the listeners to absorb the ideas

EFFECTIVE DELIVERY-THE VOICE

that you have put across. A short pause gives the audience time to absorb what you have said. You can also use pauses to help you relax and breath. Pauses also help you put your ideas together to start elaborating on a new point.

A few useful hints on the use of pauses:

- Don't feel compelled to fill the silence. If you find yourself speaking quickly for no real reason, force yourself to pause. Sometimes you may be very enthusiastic about what you are saying and find yourself speaking rapidly. Pause and use your body language and voice to show your enthusiasm

- Avoid becoming a slow speaker. Moderate the speed of your talk to the level of its contents. Always remember that the aim is to be understood and not to say as many words as possible within the given time

- Try to maintain the rhythm and the rate of flow of ideas throughout your presentation. Again this can be achieved by practicing your presentation enough times to make you feel confident and in command.

Emphasis

There are other ways to emphasize a point or an idea. The amount of stress put on a syllable can also emphasize the word. You should say certain sentences, placing emphasis on different words. A few examples are:

- Can I have that *chair* please

- Can I have *that* chair please

In the first sentence you are asking for the chair and not something else. In the second sentence, you want the chair to be given to you and not someone else. Therefore, placing the stress on a word can change the whole sentence.

Avoid putting emphasis on too many words. This diminishes the effect of the technique and renders it useless.

It is important to realize that emphasis in many cases is placed on a group of words rather than just one. The same technique applies, but in the case of a group of words, the pitch change to the decisive tone can be extended to include all the words in the group. The whole group should be treated as one entity with the emphasis on the group and not the individual words.

Voice projection

Voice projection depends on two main factors:

- Physical

- Psychological

The physical factor comprises

- The force with which you breathe

- The muscular power you put into forming the words

- The clarity of your pronunciation

If you get all these factors right then you will have no problem in projecting your voice. However, some people feel nervous in front of an audience and they fail to project their voice properly. In a lot of cases, speakers project their voices too much or too little simply

EFFECTIVE DELIVERY-THE VOICE

because they do not look at the audience and estimate the power that they need to project. In order to estimate projection, you should look at the person the furthest away from you and imagine that you are talking too him or her. You will feel the need to project your voice to that person and be able to control your vocal organs and breathing accordingly.

Use of the body

To help you to project your voice, you should make use of the resonance of your body cavities. Try the following:

- Relax the muscles in your neck and stand comfortably without bending or over straightening your chest.

- Also relax the muscles in your neck by nodding gently a few times.

- Take a deep breath and exhale, letting out a deep sound. You can then realize how the cavity in your chest resonates giving out a sigh of relief.

The nose

A clear nose helps you to speak clearly and project your voice. If your nose is blocked, it is harder for you to pronounce certain letters let alone project your voice. It is also easier to breathe through a clear nose and therefore maintain the breathing rhythm.

Improving posture

Other cavities in the body, such as the chest, can be used to create more resonance. It helps if your posture is right. For a good posture try the following:

Relax your muscles especially around the shoulder area. To do so you need to raise your shoulders and drop them a few times.

- Do not bend forward as you speak. This prevents your chest cavity from resonating

- If you stand with a curved back and too stiff you will not be able to project your voice properly

- Relax your body and stand in a natural position. This will help you not only project your voice but maintain it for a longer time too.

Training and looking after your voice

To change your speech habits which you have developed over a number of years, is not a simple matter. You need to consciously work at this before the changes become second nature to you. You should always look after your voice in order to maintain it:

- Avoid smoky rooms

- Allow your voice to rest. Even when you are giving a long talk or speech, you can still rest your voice by regular breathing and proper articulation

- Avoid warm and dry rooms which can bring on a sore throat

- Don't eat dairy products before your presentation, because the production of mucus is increased which roughens the voice

- If you feel that you have a dry mouth and throat, bite your tongue gently. This will produce enough saliva to wet your mouth.

- After a long talk, practice a few relaxing exercises to prepare your voice for rest. These exercises can be stretching, breathing articulation etc.

Now read the key points from chapter five overleaf

KEY POINTS FROM CHAPTER FIVE

- The voice plays an all important part in presentations

- It is essential to improve four characteristics of speech-tone, pitch, volume and clarity

- The use of silences and pauses is very effective when public speaking

- Voice projection is vital when speaking

- If your posture is right this enhances the ability to project your voice

CHAPTER SEVEN

EXERCISES GENERALLY

Exercises to help you relax

Although at first glance exercising may seem to have very little to do with public speaking, in fact the reverse is true. There are certain exercises which are essential to your posture and general well-being. If you are aware of these simple routines and can go through the motions just prior to embarking on public speaking, then you will feel so much better.

Shoulders

In order to feel relaxed, you should stand in a relaxed position, lift the shoulders and tense them. Slowly relax them by letting them fall. You should then note the difference in the way you feel. Sometimes we lift our shoulders and tense them without realizing that we are doing so. When your shoulders are tense, the neck becomes tense and you can feel very uncomfortable and tire more easily.

Neck

Neck exercises are very beneficial in the process of relaxation. Move your head gently round from left to right in a circular motion. Imagine that you are repeating this exercise in front of an audience. This is particularly useful for releasing tension and should be carried out just prior to beginning your presentation.

Head

In a standing position, let the head very slowly fall onto your chest. Repeat this for a few times and you feel very light and relaxed. The contrast between lightness and the heaviness which is experienced when your head is kept in a normal position over prolonged periods of time can be felt very easily.

Concentration

This particular exercise is useful for focusing the mind. Choose an interesting object that appeals to you. Fix your mind on it taking in as much detail as possible. Rest your head against the back of the chair, close your eyes and place the image of that object in your mind. When you are ready, open your eyes. Carrying out this particular exercise is useful prior to public speaking.

Breathing control

Breathing for any form of presentation is a natural function that we do not normally think about. If you find it difficult to project your voice in public, concentrating on the breathing aspects will work wonders for you.

To be heard by an audience, we need to create space in the throat and chest so that the required amount of air can be freely inhaled. When using the voice, the exhaled air is directed through the vocal cords. The throat mouth and nose help us to amplify our sound. The mouth and throat should therefore be free of tension, and the nose kept clear and unlocked for the resonators to operate effectively.

Breathing in

For this exercise, you should stand straight but not stiffly. Good posture helps promote strong voice production. Remember when you inhale not to raise the shoulders. Doing so will encourage tension in the neck, throat and breathing muscles.

Now you should feel your ribcage. Ribs form the thorax and are attached at the back to the twelve thoracic vertebrae. Rest one hand on your midriff and the other on your lower ribs that reach around the waist. Breathe in slowly and notice how the hand resting on the midriff moves out slightly. This has happened because the diaphragm, which is a muscular partition that separates the thorax from the abdomen, has contracted and flattened, thereby pushing the belly outwards. Because the lower ribs are more flexible than those higher up, they will flex outwards and upwards by the use of intercostal muscles that are attached to them.

This muscular activity expands the chest cavity, creating more space for the lungs to fill up with air, which is drawn into them through the windpipe, nose and/or mouth.

Breathing out

You should now breath out very slowly and feel the lower ribs gradually relax as the lungs contract. The diaphragm rises and the midriff or belly moves inwards. As this is happening, the abdominal muscles are gently drawn inwards. This contraction of the abdominal muscles is used to help our outgoing breath when we speak, gently supporting the diaphragm and lower ribs, so that sound can be sustained and energized.

Because it is on the outgoing breath that we speak, we aim to balance breath with sound. The moment we start to exhale, we need to use the voice. This can be achieved by humming. This will help you to attain a smoothness.

Physical tensions and feelings of nervousness can be increased or even caused by insufficient intake of air. At times, this can result in a sore throat, breathy or strained voice and tailing off at the ends of sentences. Some speakers do not allow themselves breathing space. They take in small gasps of air and do not take advantage of their breathing muscles. The shoulders may rise on inhalation, which encourages the ribs to move one way only-vertically- and this can constrict the breath. The ribs need to flex vertically and laterally. Raising the arms slightly to the side while practicing breathing in may provide a picture of opening out, so that lateral expansion is encouraged.

The voice generally

As we have discussed, when speaking in public, the voice needs to be strong and powerful without straining or shouting. You need to get the message home to people in a clear confident way. Your breath is the power behind your voice. It is important to inhale as much as possible The aim is to flow and we breath when there are pauses in the text.

In order to make sense of content, learn where to punctuate your speech and phrase your words. Do not break your phrases or your speech will become jerky and the sense may be lost.

When your speech is prepared, practice it aloud and initially gauge where you are going to take:

- Your full stop pauses

- Your comma pauses and supplementary breaths

Ensure that you are standing straight but be at ease, especially around the top part of your body, the neck, throat and shoulders, which should be relaxed and down. Stand with legs slightly apart, the weight evenly distributed on both feet. Your head needs to be well balanced between the shoulder blades. The chin should not jut out or be pushed too far into the neck. If you were speaking to a fairly large audience you would need to speak a little slower and very clearly.

The above represent a few key exercises which you should become familiar with if you wish to increase your effectiveness as a public speaker and become aware of your posture and your physical self generally.

CHAPTER EIGHT

A FEW HINTS ON SETTING

By now, you should have gained a reasonably clear idea of the ground work that you must do before you are ready to stand in front of others and deliver an effective speech or make an effective presentation. In addition, you will have gained some idea of the importance of physical exercise and its relation to your own well being. However, before you do begin your presentation it will do no harm in considering the type of environment that you will present in.

Choosing the right setting

There are a number of types of place where you may find yourself giving a presentation. These can vary from a small over ventilated room to a large and comfortable seminar room. For a good setting a room should possess the following:

- It should be large enough to accommodate all present

- The temperature should be just right and not uncomfortable (too hot or too warm)

- All seats should be positioned correctly

- Enough space should be provided for visual aids

- Lighting should be controllable

- There should be enough power points close to the location of your equipment

- The acoustics should be suitable.

If you have the chance to go into a room some time before the presentation, look out for aspects which can be improved upon and which bring the room in line with the above criteria.

Further tips are:

- Close any windows which overlook a busy street, to avoid noise pollution in the room. If the room is too warm and you need to open a window, do so before the presentation and close them just before you start

- If the room is small, with an elevated platform for the presenter to stand on, arrange the seating to give you enough space in front of the platform. Use this space and avoid standing at a higher level than your small audience. This can only intimidate them and create barriers

- If you can rearrange the seating in the room, always try to place the seats facing you with their back to the room door. This enables latecomers to sneak in without distracting peoples attention from you

- In large lecture theaters, make sure that the lighting is controlled, so that when you start your presentation, it is dimmed in the audience section. This helps the audience focus on you and your visual aids.

- However, it should not be too dark for the audience to take notes if necessary.

CHAPTER NINE

DELIVERING YOUR PRESENTATION

All that you have read has been leading to one main point: that is the day of your speech. The following should be noted in order to avoid things going wrong:

In the week before the event you should contact the organizers in order to ensure that the event is still taking place and that nothing has changed. You should ensure the following:

- You have the name and address of the venue. A simple matter but crucial

- Travel arrangements. Things such as parking and those who will meet you

- Contact name and telephone number in case you are held up on the day

- Time of the event

- Dress requirements

- Length of speech

- Names of anyone to be mentioned, for example, in a toast

- Any special facilities required by yourself should be checked beforehand

The eve of your speech

The eve of your speech is the time to check the contents of your speech, once again, and carry out any possible rehearsals. Make sure that you have checked any equipment that you are going to take with you and any visual aids. Make sure that you know what clothes you are going to wear and then try to relax. The key to the whole night before is ensuring that you have all you need, it is in working order and you are fully prepared. Then it is time to meditate. Try not to dwell on what you have to do the next day. Your subconscious is doing that for you anyway.

The day

It is essential that you give yourself enough time to reach your destination. Always leave yourself an extra half an hour so that you arrive well in advance. You will need this time to make any arrangements that are necessary prior to carrying out the speech. You will also have to meet relevant people. Before you leave for the venue make sure that you have everything with you. Check that you have things like cue cards that you may be using as a prompt. Be very careful at this point. Stop and think before you leap!

Arrival

As soon as you arrive you should make contact with the organizers and run through the running order of the day with them, establishing the start and finish times and also whether there have been any changes. At the earliest opportunity, pay a visit to the room that you will be speaking in. As we have seen, the venue is all important.

Socializing

After you have checked the venue, you may be asked to socialize. This can be a very useful time. If members of the audience see that you are mingling with them in an affable sort of way, you will reinforce the feeling that you are friendly and sympathetic and that you are interested in the people and the event. It will also take your mind off your speech and help you to judge the mood of your audience.

If you are offered a drink you should ensure that you do not get tipsy. Eat sparingly.

If you are in the room when people are taking their seats you should keep an eye on the distribution. A small audience that is scattered across a large auditorium is going to be more difficult to handle than people who are in a tight group.

A few minutes before you are due to speak, begin to prepare yourself. Make sure that you feel fresh. Take a trip to the lavatory if necessary. If you have to sit through other peoples speeches, be alert and interested. You will probably be just as visible as the person speaking and you should do nothing to distract the audiences attention. You may also need to edit your speech

When it is time to go on, and you are being introduced, look at the introducer and be alert. While the introduction is being made, breathe deeply and concentrate on the opening words of your speech. When the introduction is over, get into position, make yourself comfortable, check that you have the audiences attention, smile and begin. If you are using the same space as a previous speaker then make sure that any remnants of their speech is removed, such as chalk on blackboard etc.

Dealing with hecklers

Some people come to meetings with the sole aim of disrupting the person speaking. Others may become rowdy after drink. Dealing with such people is a key skill and totally essential if you wish to convey your message.

You should observe the audience beforehand in order to spot such people. Ignore initial heckling, attempt a witty put-down if repeated. Keep your sense of humor at all times. Demonstrate maturity and professionalism. Only if a heckler becomes extremely abusive should you think about having him or her ejected.

Question time

You may find yourself in a situation, depending on the occasion, where the audience can put questions to you. The best time for questions is when you have finished your speech so that you are not disrupted. When you take a question, listen carefully and try to repeat it. This is not only so that the audience can hear it but also so that you can frame your answer. Spend as much time as you can with questioners who are being constructive, Conversely, make sure that those who are repetitive or who ramble are stopped in their tracks.

Finally

Ensure that you stay in control at all times. Ensure that all the preliminaries have been taken care of, you are dressed correctly, you are confident, know your subject, have researched it and pieced it together well and that you grab the audiences attention. Ensure that your speech is totally relevant to the occasion.

After you have delivered your speech, irregardless of whether it has been successful or not, you will have a sense of well being.

Good luck with your maiden speech.

Now read the key points from chapter eight overleaf.

KEY POINTS FROM CHAPTER EIGHT

- Contact the organizers one week before the event in order to ensure that all is running smoothly and that you are still speaking

- On the eve of your speech, carry out rehearsals in order to get yourself in the right state of mind

- Give your self plenty of time to reach your destination

- If you socialize prior to your speech, ensure that you do not drink too much

- When you embark upon your speech, ensure that you know how to handle the audience, in particular how to handle hecklers

- Ensure that you allow time for questions after

- Above all, relax!

CHAPTER TEN

SOCIAL EVENTS AND SPEECHES

In this chapter, we will look at events in which you will most likely find yourself invited to speak. The most common are weddings and work related functions. However, sometimes you may find yourself invited to compere an event or to act as master of ceremonies. In addition, you could find yourself in the position where you have to give an impromptu speech. The key to all speeches is being well prepared and to be self confident. These have been the central messages of this book.

In this chapter, I do not offer sample speeches. Although many books do, I have found that they neglect all the other aspects of delivering a speech, such as the essential preparation. Instead, I will cover the essence of the event and offer a few tips on structuring speeches.

1. The Compere

A compere does not usually make or give speeches. He or she will introduce others and will "warm up" the audience. This is the role most closely associated with show business and the person undertaking it will usually be a comedian The role is similar to master of ceremonies, in that you have to ensure that everything goes smoothly without taking over the show. Like the master of ceremonies, the role of the compere demands good timing and the ability to ensure that all goes smoothly between one speaker and another.

2. Master of ceremonies

A master of ceremonies is employed by the organizer of an event to ensure that all the stages of the event go smoothly and the event is a success.

The MC does not organize the event. The key role is that of liaison person between all those participating. The MC will also act as troubleshooter ensuring that any last minute problems are resolved. At a formal dinner, the MC will introduce everyone and propose a toast as necessary. They will make connections between one speaker and another, just as a person making a speech will link the various elements of the speech.

The content of a MC's speeches is information. The MC must therefore be concise and to the point and make sure that all the facts are right. This role is not the easiest of roles and most people do not appreciate just how much work goes into it. The role can be a learning curve for the budding public speaker, however. The MC can practice the art of impromptu speaking and there is the opportunity to deal with various audience types, and the moods of the audience.

After dinner speaking

Almost all after dinner speeches take the form of toasts and replies. In certain cases, a guest speaker will also have been invited, and in this case an introduction will be given.

It will normally fall to the chair of the occasion to see that the list of toasts and speakers is drawn up, and that each speaker is introduced in the correct order. Whoever is in control of the proceedings it is essential that they have a sense of timing and brevity. He or she should know how to speed things up or slow things down or put things back on course.

Proposing a toast

Toasts are intended as a celebration or as well wishing. They should be kept brief and upbeat, optimistic without sycophancy or self congratulation. When proposing a toast you should try to begin with humor or an anecdote. Replying to a toast is a little more complicated, in that it requires the speaker to respond to the proposer as well as a short speech. Listen carefully to what the proposer is saying and think on your feet.

The system of toasts and response make it possible for comments to be passed to and fro. If the speakers are skilled at this then the outcome can be very entertaining. However, you should resist at all costs the temptation to enter into dispute with other speakers. This will only ruin the occasion and often make you look silly and unprofessional.

When preparing a speech at a dinner, make sure that you do your homework. You will need to know the names of relevant people and you will need to have something to say which is relevant to the occasion. Do not get carried away by your own eloquence and make sure that you remember to propose a toast.

Introducing a guest speaker

Some organizations engage a guest speaker, someone who may be connected with the organization or who may have something of special interest to say. If you are asked to introduce the guest speaker, make sure that you find out who he or she is and why they have been invited. From this point, when introducing the speaker, you can ensure that the person and the event are connected.

The main object of an after dinner speakers appearance is to be amusing and the major imperative is to be relevant to the occasion and topical. The brief is normally very wide ranging. If you are in this position, then you should make sure that you have researched your topic well and that you understand the audience. The conditions under which many after dinner speeches are given are quite often difficult. The audience may be on the way to inebriation, may be scattered around the room, on some occasions loutish. This means that you will have to work very hard and keep the occasion under control.

Weddings

For many people, there are only a few occasions when you will need to make a speech. The most common of these are business and weddings.

At weddings, it is customary to have three speeches, all of which are toasts. The first is proposed by the father of the bride, or a close family friend or relative. He or she will propose the health of the bride and groom. Next, the groom will reply and proposes a toast to the bridesmaids. Finally, the best man will reply on behalf of the bridesmaids.

Each of these speeches should be prepared in advance and delivered as a normal speech.

The toast to the bride and groom should express happiness at the occasion and wish them both luck in their future life. It is customary to compliment the bride on her appearance and congratulate the groom on his luck. You may wish to draw on anecdotes from your past with one of the participants or you may want to tell a funny story. Finish by asking the guests to raise their glasses in a toast to the couple.

You should never make the bride or groom the butt of a joke. This is ignorance and will cause severe embarrassment. Never make remarks in bad taste, avoid smut or innuendo and avoid scandal. Remember, this is a day to remember for the bride and groom and also the family and not an occasion to embarrass others. If you do that, you will reveal yourself as a sad and rather pathetic figure.

After the toast to the bride and groom will come the toast to the bridesmaids. The groom will thank the previous person proposing a toast and will compliment the bride on her appearance and comment on his good fortune at having found her. He will thank the best man for supporting him. Sometimes, the groom will also thank the brides family. However, not surprisingly, women sometimes frown on this as it implies that they are possessions to be passed on. A few anecdotes will go down well from the groom and he will finish by proposing a toast to the bridesmaid.

The Best Man

The best mans speech is usually the highlight of the occasion. The audience is expecting a humorous speech and one that will last five to ten minutes. The best man will start by thanking the groom on behalf of the bridesmaids. Something is said about the relationship with the groom and to tell some stories about your past together. The groom may be embarrassed on this occasion, however his reputation should remain intact.

Never make jokes in bad taste. Always keep your audience in mind. Avoid excess alcohol before the speech. Do not make lewd comments. At the end, read out any congratulations by way of telegram or letter.

Because the best mans speech is the longest, it is essential that the best man co-ordinates the speeches making sure that they synchronize.

It is also very important, and it has been stressed throughout this book, that the best man, indeed all those who deliver speeches, is confident and in control, thereby engendering confidence in others. There is nothing worse than the sight of a nervous speaker. People cringe and wait for something to go wrong.

Impromptu speaking

There may be occasions when you will be invited, out of the blue, to give a speech off the cuff, without preparation. Many people dread when being called on to speak. Minds start to go blank and people become acutely self conscious. The key to this is to simply get up and start speaking. Think quickly.

In many respects this is the same problem you face when working on a prepared speech. The solutions are basically the same. The main question is: what do I want to achieve? The first component is a central thought, something around which to gather other points. There may be no particular purpose in mind on such an occasion, except to amuse. In this case you might want to talk about the audience or the occasion You could always pick up on a remark made by another speaker.

If you have a professional background and it is relevant to the occasion start by stating your credentials. This focuses peoples minds. Don't go on too long. If you do you will lose track and you could start to bore others. Don't speak too quickly. Again, as has been emphasized, self confidence and self assuredness are the keys to successful speaking.

Keynote speeches

Certain people are invited, quite frequently, to deliver keynote speeches at the opening of events or exhibitions. The speeches that they give encapsulate the essence of the event. This is why these particular speeches are important.

If you are asked to give a keynote speech, find out as much as you can about the event. If it is a conference for example, find out who the other speakers are and what themes will be covered. You will be able to get this information from the organizers.

- Find out who the event is aimed at

- Formulate a statement of the purpose of the event

- Begin by welcoming everyone and thanking the organizers for inviting you. Tell the audience the main theme of the event and give your thoughts. Tell them what the main aims of the event are and why they are important.

- In conclusion, you may like to wish all participants success and encourage everyone to enjoy the event.

Do not forget:

- For the speechmaker, preparation and audience understanding are everything

- Self confidence and assertiveness are vital elements. Without these you will never remain in control

Good luck!

OTHER STRAIGHTFORWARD GUIDES

Other guides in the series:

A Straightforward Guide to:

The Rights of the Private Tenant
Small Claims in the County Court
Teaching your child to Swim
Divorce and the Law
Personal finance
Accounts and Book-keeping for Small business
Business Planning
Teaching Your Child to Read and Write
Caring for a Disabled Child
Creative writing
Freelance Writing
Writing Romantic Fiction
How to Write and Market your own Screenplay
Family Law
Taking your own Legal Action
Buying a used Car
Get Home Safely-Guide to surviving Motoring Emergencies
Century Guides:
Stately Homes
Car Museums
Railways
Gardens
Alternative Health
Computing
Self Defence
Raising a Child
The Straightforward C.V
Bankruptcy and Insolvency
Setting up a Business

Speech writing
Negotiations
The Bailiff and You-The law
The Rights of the Consumer
Effective Leadership
Effective Time Management
Effective management
The Rights of the Leaseholder
Marketing Explained
Effective Marketing
Effective Presentations
Performance Poetry
The Alexander Technique
Stress Management
Guide to Tiling for beginners
How to do your own Conveyancing
Buying and selling a Home
Carrying out a Structural Survey
Letting Property for Profit
Taking legal action-What to Expect in Court
Getting the best out of your Solicitor
Guide to Employment Law

If you would like to comment on this publication or would like to contribute to Straightforward Guides then please write to:

Straightforward Publishing
38 Cromwell Road
walthamstow
London, E17 9JN

Tel: 0181 521 6168